Mourning

MOURNING

A Collection of Poems

Written and Illustrated by
Erin Browning

ISBN: 979-8-218-29736-7 (Paperback)
Library of Congress Control Number: : 2023920211

Any references to historical events, real people, or real
places are used fictitiously. Names, characters, and places
are products of the author's imagination.

Cover photograph and interior photographs by
Karim Badwan. Book design by Erin Browning and
Heidi Reynolds.
Typeset by Felicia Cedillos.

Printed by Ingram Sparks Inc., One Ingram Blvd. La
Vergne, TN 37086 in the United States of America. First
printing edition 2023.

Published by Erin Browning, Melrose, MA.

Contents

Acknowledgements

When we feel we have no other choice, we dig deep.
This is the space where magic happens.

I am first and foremost grateful for the conundrum of living a
love filled life.

For the unconditional love that started this book, I thank Dave
Smoot. You set it all up. You loved me in ways I didn't know
were possible. You let me love both you and your son. You left as
powerfully as you came into a room (or my life). The timing of
it all… you declared it "the end" before I was ready to turn the
page. Your exit left me with no choice but to live and write the
truth.

For the creativity that came next, I thank the following people.
Heidi Reynolds, your patience and guidance as my creative
coach and book designer is invaluable. Candace Cook, our
reconnection reminded me of childhood which allowed me to
write from a place less logical than I had planned. Suz Leigh,
the depth of your acceptance of my ideas might be coo coo or
it might be genius, either way I am glad our paths cross as they
do. The Ohio Hudsons, you all believed in me before I did. Your
girls reminded me I was capable and of the value in running a
good creative experiment.

For the steadiness and support, I thank my Mom (Debbie) and Stepdad (Alan), my Aunt Becky, my sister Laci, Sue, and the rest of my family and chosen family who stepped in (too many of you to list). You let me be right in the messy middle even when you wanted to see me on the other side.

For the reminder that love is always worth it, I thank Karim. Your ability to reflect the light is one of a kind, literally and metaphorically. I appreciate your partnership creatively on this book. I am even more grateful for how we are co-creating this journey of life together.

For the magic, I give extra special thanks, to free will. When our choices come from love we can't go wrong.

Some events change us.
We wake to a normal day,
living a typical life,
we blink our eyes open
and everything is different.
In an instant life becomes unrecognizable.

Three years ago, just before midnight, I watched the person I thought I'd spend the rest of my life with take his last breath. Life changed in that instant. It no longer made sense. Day after day I kept going. Every morning I wrote.

Words allowed me to make sense of the unsensible.

This collection of expressions is an intimate account of my thoughts, feelings, and beliefs discovered during this transition from love to grief and back to love.

I hope by reading this you will explore the moments of life that are mostly unutterable. I hope you will see the magic, mystery, & sacredness that comes by staying open to all life offers. I hope you will see the bravery in loving someone completely.

Most of all I hope you with every "I" written on the pages
you feel seen and heard in the common human experience of unraveling.

Raw Delusion

get in it
the messiness
of my human life

allow
let the fire
melt me
instead of burn me
to the ground

wrap myself up
in love
knowing full well

there may be a day
all that pleases
and satiates the gaps
is gone again

it's a gorgeous disaster
my heart holds
completely

One week. One hour.
Telling the story of my wholeness as a human.

Not a broken being. A human.
It is all because of love.
I was loved. I am loved

Done with the old story of hurt, pain, mistreatment that caused
me to believe I was anything
less than exactly who I need to be for this lifetime.
This story is being written—right now.
The old one is no longer welcome in my mind, body, or heart.

I am here fully.
No choice but to be.
Pain presents possibility.
Every single cell in me
loveable and valuable.

Infinite love around me. What's gone is gone and what's left is
love.

There is more to come in the stability of knowing the type of
love that scoops me up, shows me the truth, allows me to burn,
melt even, and rise back up again.

Held
writes this story.
Love
writes this story.

Cocoon

It is when the old body dies. Protected by a layer of silk the new
body forms.

Right now
pleasure fleeting
at best, peace non-existent

escape the world of reality in the slowest hours of dark
MORNING
and MOURNING.

I dip into the changes happening in my cocoon.
Something new.
My old body holds onto what was.

Stroking my skin as if weaving the tender strong silk around me.
Stretching my limbs in the most peculiar of motions.
Changing.
Lost and held.

The configuration of who I was, who I have always been
dying.
I can feel it.
Loving myself
all that's left.

My mind holds more tightly.
Control the process.
I can't—
even try
not a single part of this event is in my control.
An event.
If death can be simplified into a life event this can be simplified
into a metamorphosis.

Love.
That's all.
My purest essence is love—no rearrangement.
Now is all there is.

So be it.
Right now
before the peep of light
practice love
let love lead inevitable changes to come.

Stay Wild

Here at the river's edge
Ice daunting
sun peeking through

I'm safe.
I'm here.
You're gone.
Words don't often escape me but
today
All in.
All in my body.
My heart.
My senses.

You lived there.
You taught me this.
(gave me permission to live it myself)

Fog rolling out.
Toes freezing.
But I am breathing.

Just breathe.
You told me that once.
Breathe.

More than once
I knew *you saw me*

The wild you love
Is still here
I'll keep finding her
You keep coming to me
Please

Don't let my living drive you away

There is room for it all
if we just follow the love
through the freezing flow of this river

Why did you leave? *I have no idea sweetheart*
Can you come every night? *I can't. It isn't healthy for you or for me.*

Healthy for you?
What?
You are dead.

He is dead.

For now, I'll pretend, in this little chasm of my creation, only
light. None of the shame that bound us both in life. None of
the complications of family–responsibilities–decisions. None of
the angst of trying to figure out this life or the former we had
together. He holds me.

We melt until I fall back asleep.

Enveloped in the brightest white glow.

I beg him for the answers.
I did not ask for this– so why am I here?
Shouldn't he know? Why won't he clue me in– so I can rest for a
few minutes of the longest span of time I've known in my life.

Was all of it my overactive imagination? *Always too sensitive.
Unrealistic.*

How do I rectify this world and the normal world?

Repeating   Repeating   Repeating

Walking into the kitchen, boiling the water, pouring it over the
coffee that I used to believe was delicious.

Now there is nothing delicious left.

What might satisfy is
to have the light back.
to stay in the cavern of time I have dreamed up.
to have the solution to this goddamned problem
to get one tasty sip, only one, that warms me from the inside out
and reminds me it might be ok.

There are no answers and the problem cannot be fixed.

Between sleep and wake

I close my eyes to an overwhelming glow

A stroke? Only if it takes me.
Turn away. It's everywhere.
Impossible.

I feel him.

Sense him in the room.
He is here.

I believed. I knew.

Sun up and bitter cold. Eyes open.
The entire night was a lie.
My imagination.
Lost again. Complete devastation.

I can't push my way through the stretchy walls holding me
together, but preventing my breath.

I want the fuck out. No way out.

This is real. Here and now.

Can I scream?
It is too hard.

A boomerang
comes and smacks me
in the face
with force of his death
again, and again, and again

I woke. I remembered.

Every morning, back here
the ones left have sad eyes, weird grimacing faces.
Pity it seems and I hate pity.
Can I run?
The only one that matters is gone.
He is gone.
The white opaque hue so bright I thought it would take me.
Can I find it?

I have no peace.

Not even close.
Here and vanished.
Quick as he exited that night.

It is done

me
pulled
into D's world
done now

me
dragging
him into our world

stop now

so I can live

Veils

thinned
at the start and
at the end

of life—

no more than an exhale between where we are and what we
don't know
like a window cracked—slither through
explore

a quick slip
able to see beyond

through the transparent fracture
time is limited

clear sight
soon to become opaque blocks
blade sharp edges   pigmented colors   curves
angles—depths of every texture—penetrate my heart

blurry understanding
remembering   becoming   forgetting   unbecoming

transformation in a liminal space
alive—sensual

I can breathe here
I can feel here
no room for anything
but truth

exhaustive acceptance
of all that
was and is
was not and is not

allows me
to love me
find me
to be

in the space between the worlds
where it ends
where it begins
again

Preparation

Remember

I re-membered my center
me as love
for 47 checked out minutes each night
before I drift to a drug induced sleep.

Praying starts with ritual,
performed when I was a little girl

Our Father who art in heaven, hallowed be thy name, thy
kingdom come, thy will be done, on earth as it is in heaven…

desperate times
call for rearrangement

My own version

a grown woman's call
…then I took a breath, touched HER tenderness

Her will be done
Her love be embraced
Her mind
Her soul
CAPABLE
to shuffle the pieces of this reality
remember the past and emerge into everything
she
needs to be

SHE
ALREADY
IS

All of me.
For me.

It is not a flaw
to choose to love

My heart
My mind
My determination
My words
My communication
My openness
My love
My patience
My willingness to participate
My forgiveness
My smiles and laughter
My playfulness
My loyalty
My kindness
My compassion
My sensuality
My creativity

A choice
To love my humanness
Yours too
When I miss the mark
I am still here

Loving.
Loveable.
Loved.

part of reality sinks in
I don't want it.
a sense of love leaving
a hazy notion of this new me

I don't know her

Yet…

the red hot yearning
always

signifies rising
my opportunity

loosen the bind
allow air in
let it all burn
disintegrate into ash

yet the ghost of him is less terrifying than new growth peeking
through charcoal crust

left by destruction of our heart's fire

lose the sacred
lose the connection
check with reality
what was
what is
Let the smoke burn my eyes and remember I can see

I am left here to live
in truth
lean into the colorless ash covering every surface of my life
Ascend

Reality → is irreverant

what good is glorifying yesterday?

I can hold dear the finished
and live here too.

Reality → is irreverant

Bound

Only one way to know what's real.

Feel inside the edges.
Move my awareness into my center.
Sync breath and body.

You do the same. We are close. We watch one another. Your
breath syncs with mine.

Reality in the concentrated vessel of myself.
I know
what is real
acknowledge you
honor me.

curious

curious if you bailed on life because it was heartbreaking to feel
it disintegrate

the heat
my hands
your heart
too much

the failing structure you bought into for 55 years
you were dismantling your mind

but your body couldn't take it
there we were

no turning back
limbs heavy
lifeless body
dead weight
bigger than life
smoldered into nothing

my hands
on your heart
you bailed

your clear proclamation
fly beyond these suffocating mountains

unspoken
live with an invisible tether
lover

I loosened that cord
pulling strand by strand

truth—
you couldn't stand it
you said you wanted it and me
no
hated it
and sometimes
me

staying silent
you needed to scream
our brand of love would not hold up
in this revolution of my soul

here
I fight the urge to think
the unraveling
is why you died

Did my desire for more kill you?

stifled bellows
clogging your heart
TRUTH sparked
caught fire
not the good
light you up type

uncontrollable
whole heart on the table

or floor

burn it down sort

this me

you could not
you and your strength

scared little boy ways
powering through it

you would have bucked

a feral horse
terrified
of a tiny sight
a minute sound
shaking up
false security

my voice
my words
fear —   dictating you
YOU —   dictating
nothing
any longer
you asked for it

brave and bold
no wambly pambly lady
follow me blindly
can't you just get behind me

NOPE.

not when

You.
Are.
Dead.
Wrong.

you picked a hillbilly girl
suited your needs right
RIGHT?
the hills are in my bones

but
this mtn mama
is more than a
follow you into the holler

have a swig of shine
stand by
her man
kind

Rising

Higher than the ditch you pulled me from
Disturbed your world

You saw it coming—seeing things is your power
truth is, You were only a man
Not so powerful

Your sharp words & strong ideas— melting

At the touch
Of My Heat Rising

You thought you were invincible

Wanted to be my superhero
Hell NO.
Broken bones I knew you that way
Long Ago

Broken body
Broken heart
Proved your fragility

Learned that lesson, Didn't you?
Dead on the floor

Rising
Collapsing

No choice—I carry on

Is it real?
this urgency

such a short time
HERE

every single drive, move, hike, meal, call, photo, flight, cry, song,
kiss, hug, party, date, dance, swim, run, cab ride, book read, word
written, breath taken
fuck.
right here
it all needs to count

for something

it does
it informs

washes over every part of me
the warm undercurrent submerges

go
under

cry, scream, collapse,
laugh, smile, sigh,
delight in it
live in it

leave
soar

we both fly
landlocked no more

Escape

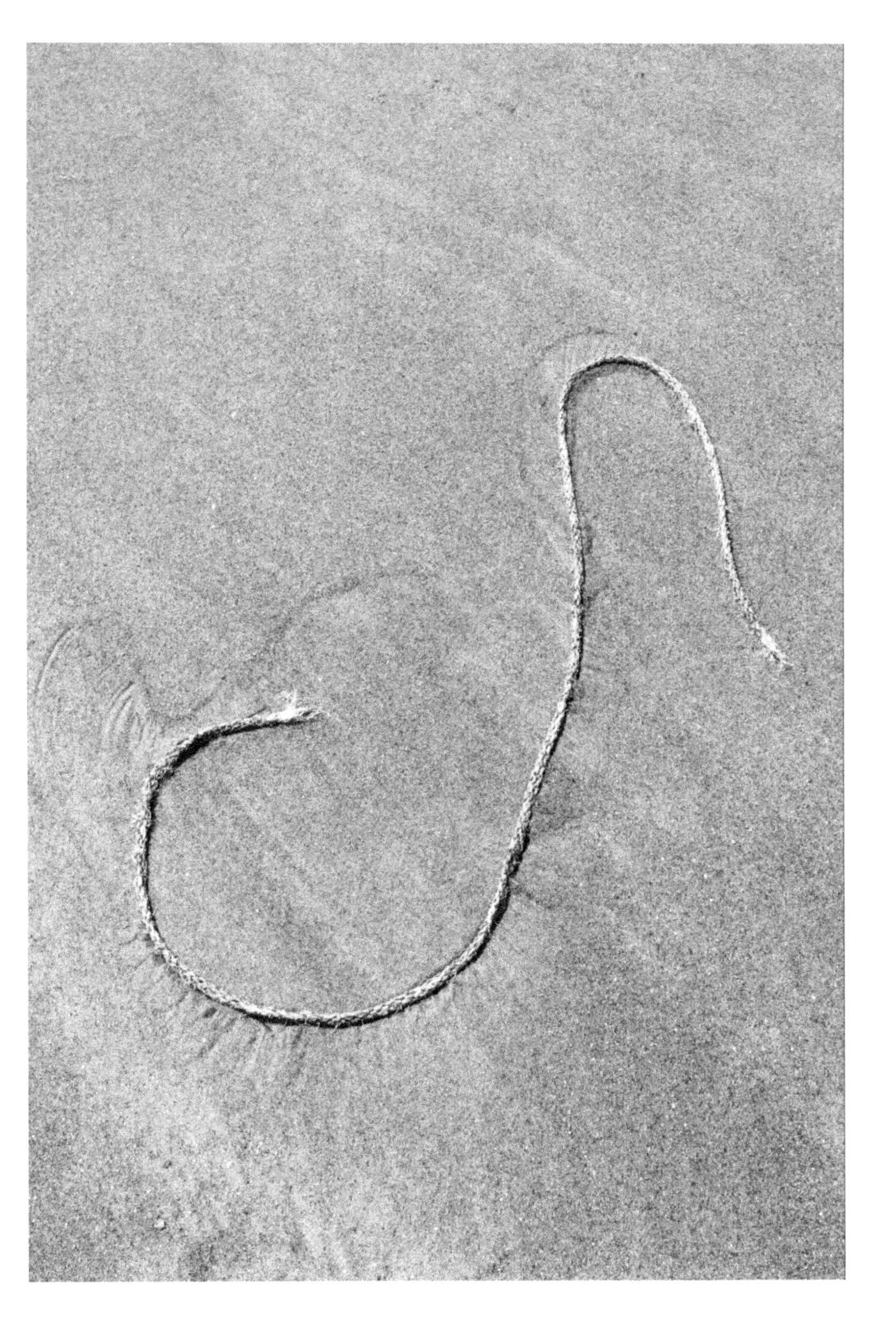

Moving forward

they say.

there I said it too

or
changing
living

knowing the shift
frightens me.

opening up
to life
the more I let in
the more I feel

no space inside me

suffocating
smothering
in this abyss

so I
walk
walk
walk
some more

pain in my chest eases so slightly as tears fall down
body moves with feet on the pavement
carrying on
the slowest
momentum
imaginable
moving forward

terrified

Running from it all

I did run
from the Gods
and THE God
with a guns and feuds and fence lines
narrative

ridiculous country song
but it's real there

construed drama
bibles believed in and babies neglected
grandmas sitting in the porch swing
at the head of the holler
and grandaughters begging to get the fuck out

I can't recall the good
not vividly
pretty hills and poor people
hearts of gold and ideas of decay

stuck
mired in corruption
wanting out but not so much that I stayed away

I hate the world for bringing me there

mom too
dad for not leaving

angry
not going far enough
not being good enough

running again
seething in shame

if I get out
it won't last

cut it off
at the pass
before
it sucks me
back again

run far and hard and fast

Renavigation

My intuition guides
My heart thumps
Find the exact balance
My mind is a mess
It goes off the trail

I am startled by the bark of a dog
I sob at the beauty of every flower
the curve of a rock and texture of each tree
Seconds later sobs stop and I marvel
at the very same experiences with a smile

Go Slow

Don't Stop

I've been at a halt long enough
Ease into it
Put one damn foot in front of the other

Allow it all.

Begging to heal

Hot sands. Shifting
So am I.

Prickly cactus. One tiny touch and it hurts like hell.
Change poking.
Trying to draw blood at every single turn.

Heat stirs within.
Up the brown mountains,
rocks everywhere, feet slipping.

The blue sky teases, looking down. Devour.

Swallow me up sky.

Loss engulfing…

Sitting in the cold house alone, gazing through the
skylight into a gray swarm of clouds just over the cold
spot where he died

…yet to consume my soul.

Details clear
on the trail exploring
they hit me
quick present moment bursting in.

Every whisper of the wind, uneven terrain,
blisters rubbing.
Beads dripping from my brow

chill comes when the sun goes down
sweat still painted

like his love used to be

all over my skin

Reminds me
I am alive.

Tears

Every single time
I drive

Hand on the wheel
mind frayed

Part sad
I can't make life work

Part numb
I can't let tears come

safe keeping
in
mourning
barely
beneath
the surface

Crying
when I am alone
not because I am lonely

but afraid
It will be good

Go far

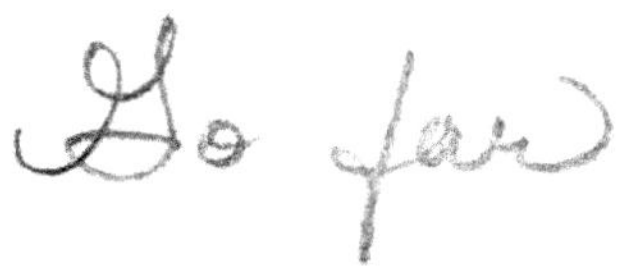

far enough to turn off the noise

hear the breeze
hoping
my imagination doesn't blow it into a tornado knocking me
down

go that distance.

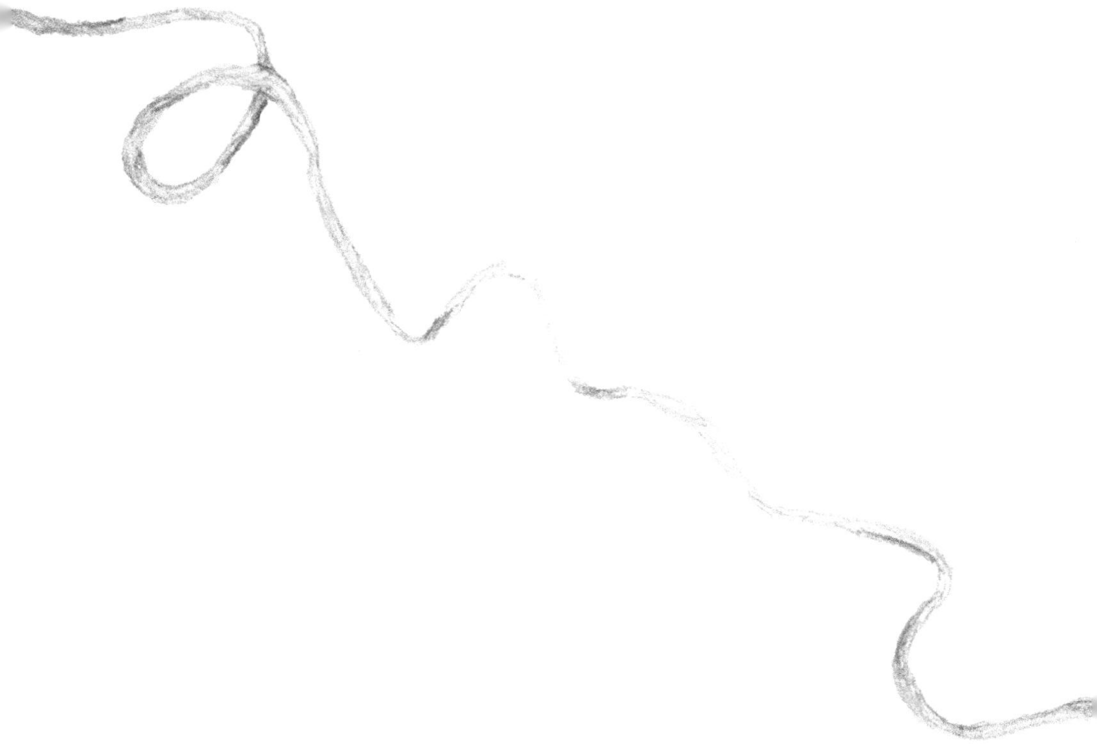

These damned desert trails are not as clearly marked as the
woods back home.

Why aren't they more clearly marked?
Oh a reality check on my life.
Why isn't life more clearly marked?
Oh, but it is.

Marked with moments that take us to our knees.
Marked with moments that lift us up to turn a joyous flip in the eye
of the storm.
I found both with him.
And again on this earth right now.
It is all inside of me.

I beg the ache of my heart to dial back its potency
the ache of this body will guide my way
as it moves from one action to the next
breathe

I may never experience the sweet juiciness of life again. I'm
longing for nectar that feeds, absorbed into every cell of my
body, my mind, my heart.

I am already here. The sweetness tastes different.

I don't want it yet.

Adventure reminds me
I DO get the most delicious sip
from time to time.

Maybe it is living.
One step at a time.
The noise turns into quiet

healing
nourishing
loving

Still here

Loss isn't gone

It hangs on.
A tick that has latched trying to take the blood.

Drawing away my life force.

There aren't any ticks here in the desert.
I let go of the parasites when loss bit.

Still here, burrowing in my heart

Where all Should be well

anticipated music
I've looked forward

in a group of hippies
melancholy washes over
my eyes scan
see the ease of their laughter
smoothness in their movements
exhilaration other people feel

I don't

heart thumps
hands tremble
breath jumps
tears well

I want to be dead
but I don't want to kill myself
I want to celebrate
I've gotten this far

and I can't allow myself
to shake (it)

to let the beat
tip my body into a chasm
of permissible happiness
let alone

pleasure
love
Joy

The widow's voice

Her voice cracks
This time not mine

                          tiny wail full of fear & pain

My tears flow to the rhythm of her gasps

The thought that all this love could live right in me
In my battered up heart
My mind cannot conceive it

And somehow
I am allowing my heart
My mind
My life
To open again

I gasp
I sob
I expand
I love

Changed

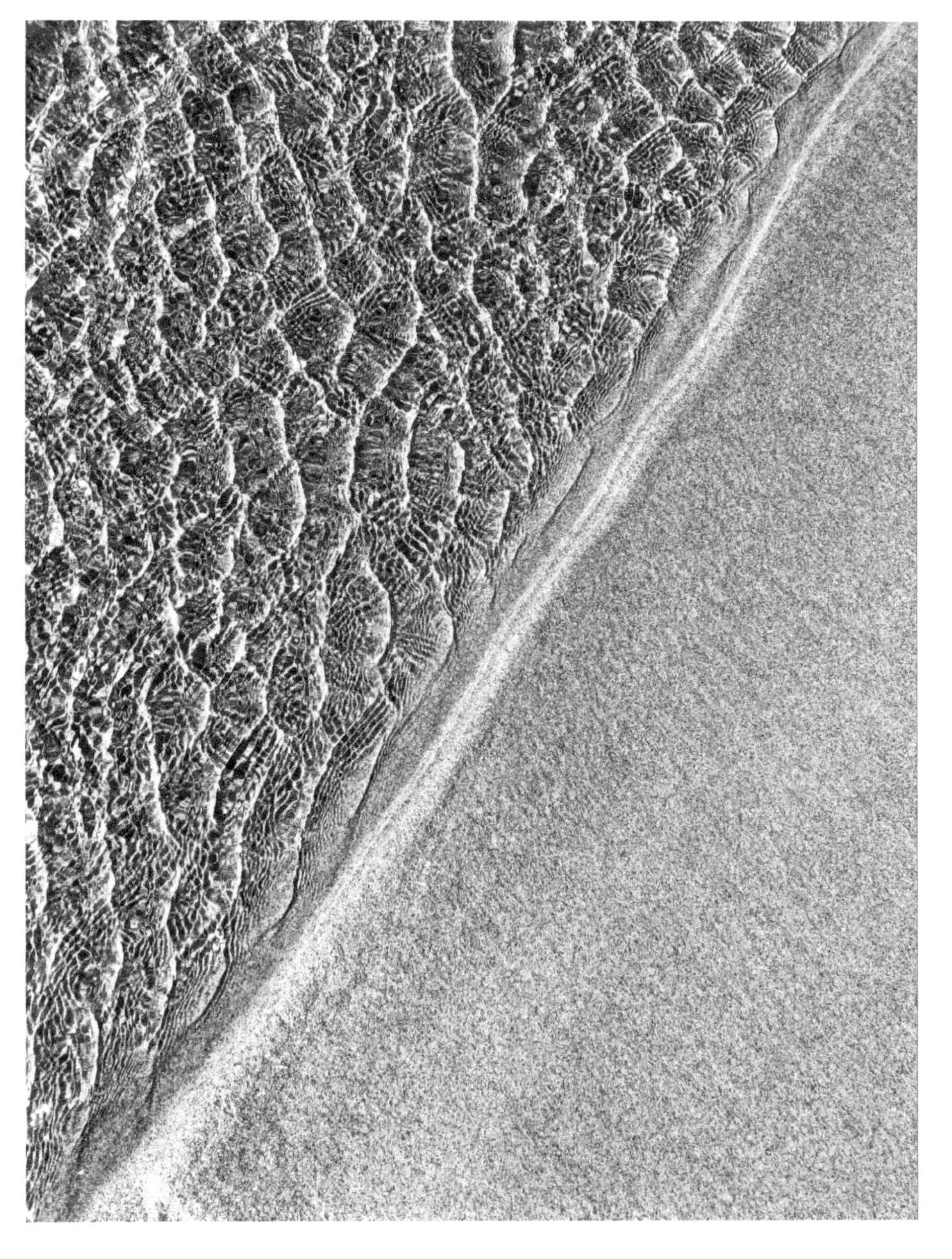

There is light

But no tunnel

No end
No through

Only a new reality
Here and now

Let go

in this moment all I had left was
conceding to
the warmth of my skin.

my own arms wrapping this body
one hand clinging to my aching ribs
the other grasping onto the sturdiness of my hip bone

my own touch
staving off my broken heart
so forceful
it explodes me from the inside out
slow down
soften
settle the fray

Live day to day
In a way
I didn't ask for

Out of control
Run with it
Not from it

I didn't ask
For this

And the
Only way
Is
Open

Sleepless

Words flowing

Leaving me reeling
And rejoicing

In this space
I forget
to write them
In this state
I forget
Me

She who
Creates
Moves
Hopes
Giggles & cries
freely

goes away
when she is not alone

Remembering doesn't work

uncertain
how to
be here
be me

confused
she is new
never existed before

disoriented
she is being born
or unborn

exhausted
trying to return
to someone
who doesn't exist

magic
on some slow mornings
there's a space
she exists

I remember
beyond what is stored
from the past
in my mind

retrieving
or is it
reviving
the soul

control is lost
letting go leads me to wholeness
again and again

wildness
in the moment
complete presence with experience unfolding

How out of control is that?

easier when I am in my body
mired down in the story it's lost

the wildness comes through me
when I am in nature,
when I slather in oil—hair to pink toes & step into
a hot shower so it slides off my skin,
when I hear the music so fully I forget what I am
supposed to be singing,
when I write,
when I stretch or dance with no agenda,
when I walk without purpose,
when I laugh deep from my belly with a friend,
when I step my bare feet onto the grass & feel the
cold mud hold me up,
when I taste the ginger on my lips from a hot cup
of tea after a day of salty tears

embrace the wild
save me
find me

Single breath
laughter rose up from nowhere
I noticed the boulder pressing on my heart ease up
I was certain I'd feel joy again

Small step
feet began to steady under me even on shaky ground
I took a step, then another, forward motion
I was sure I'd know capable again

Quickest blink
eyes focused, as did my brain
the words written on the pages stuck
I was confident I'd soon do more than survive

Sharp turn
tears stopped pouring
peace came for the next hour
I was confident I'd soon do more than survive

Mind drift
brain dreamed up a goal
not just a way to heal but a way to help
I was clear I'd find purpose

Sweet moment
smile stayed
it was a tiny bit wider than the sadness.
I knew the love I felt could live and grow
right alongside the grief

Swift stroke
head popped up from a cold ocean dip
gasping
a dreary day but my insides felt warmed
I was positive that I was making my way to whole

New
transformed
altered and complete
my thoughts absorbed
comprehending this life
As me

Unanswerable questions

Can living unwind what binds me?

Relearning
Repatterning
No effort
No therapy
No talking

Can life change my brain's chosen routes?

presence
softening the synaptic fires
the explosions in the back of my brain
that set me up
for tears

The dying
The living
All ok.
I think?

Last unanswerable…
I Promise.

How has my brain, my body
found a way to allow this

mess

trauma

to morph into something freeing?

pointed consistency

see here
feel here
be here

reliability
I see it
clearly
briefly

through the murky
web of loss

torn open soul
oppressive load
laborious pulling
every direction, no direction

Look
Look
Look

where did it go

it's real
as the sameness of cold autumn rain
and fallen leaves
every single year

love
searching for a space
to touch in

it's here
in me
even in mourning

breathe
find it
follow it
caress it
believe it

Right Here

love

the only
line through

Hold on if you can

stay wild

he loved you that way
Wait
Wait
Wait

You're missing it babes.

YOU
LOVE
YOU
this way.

I am so goddamned lucky

all of this love in me

immeasurable fortune
essentiality
that allows me

to say yes to life again

reality here and now

She is different now

wearing cardigans the color of skittles
letting the grey grow in
wild & gorgeous

silk tree
invading the forest

stays put and firm instead of fading
into her mind
sleeping at the turn of the hour

sets herself free
when need be

looks for the cloud cover
the sun
hopes the rain soaks her bones
her heart warm enough
to melt the ice as it pelts her skin in the harsh winter

she cuts you loose too
        often not so gracefully

feels

into the pit of her belly

trusts

herself

desires

to trust
the world
goodness of humans

She tries a little harder now
sometimes doesn't try at all

wrongs and rights

None of it
Constant or
Relevant

this new woman

Do I even like her?
I wonder

Would you have liked her?
Of course but does it matter

Tender skin
Elongated spine
Widened mouth
Bellowing wails of
laughter

truths

She seeks now
Something greater than her chasm of need

Moving on
forward
outgrown

(*who she was*) through

Time
Love
Escape
Opinions
Distance
Closeness
Living

I know I love her.

Making weird marks
Writing senseless words onto this page

Tolerant
Considerate
of herself
finding the grace to give in

She is different.

Melding
What was
what is

Her past
Her lineage

Then I felt it

HER

Fierce —- Sweet
Angry — Contracted
Awake — Exhausted
Alive — Open

skin crawls
looking back

Pause

Breathe

mind rattles
looking forward

Pause

Breathe

She is new

HERE

caressing curves
exploring edges
following lines
of

LOVE

through
every
gasp
retreat
rise

in awe
unknown

She changed